ALL ABOUT DINOSAURS

T. REX

BookLife

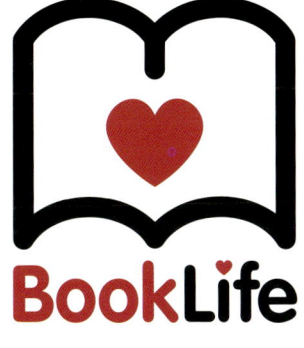

by
Amy Allatson

©2017
Book Life
King's Lynn
Norfolk PE30 4LS

ISBN: 978-1-78637-041-9

All rights reserved
Printed in Malaysia

Written by:
Amy Allatson

Edited by:
Charlie Ogden

Designed by:
Drue Rintoul

A catalogue record for this book is available from the British Library.

PHOTO CREDITS

Abbreviations: l-left, r-right, b-bottom, t-top, c-centre, m-middle.

Front Cover - metha1819. 2 - Kostyantyn Ivanyshen. 4 - iurii. 6 - robin2. 8background - Photobank gallery. 4 - 2j architecture. 10 - kridsada tipchot. 11 - JIANG HONGYAN. 12 - First Step Studio. 14background - Alexandra Lande. 14 - DM7. 15 - Herschel Hoffmeyer. 16background - Alexandra Lande. 16 - Elle Arden Images. 17t - Linda Bucklin. 17b - Sofia Santos. 18background - Iakov Kalinin. 18l - MarcelClemens. 18r - guysal. 19 - Marques. 20 - metha1819. 22 - wawritto. 23 - nathapol HPS. Images are courtesy of Shutterstock.com.
With thanks to Getty Images, Thinkstock Photo and iStockphoto.

CONTENTS

PAGE 4 What Were Dinosaurs?
PAGE 6 When Were Dinosaurs Alive?
PAGE 8 Tyrannosaurus Rex
PAGE 10 What Did the Tyrannosaurus Rex Look Like?
PAGE 12 Where Did the Tyrannosaurus Rex Live?
PAGE 14 What Did the Tyrannosaurus Rex Eat?
PAGE 16 Was the Tyrannosaurus Rex the Biggest Dinosaur?
PAGE 18 How Do We Know…?
PAGE 20 Facts About the Tyrannosaurus Rex
PAGE 22 Draw Your Own Dinosaur
PAGE 23 Glossary
PAGE 24 Index

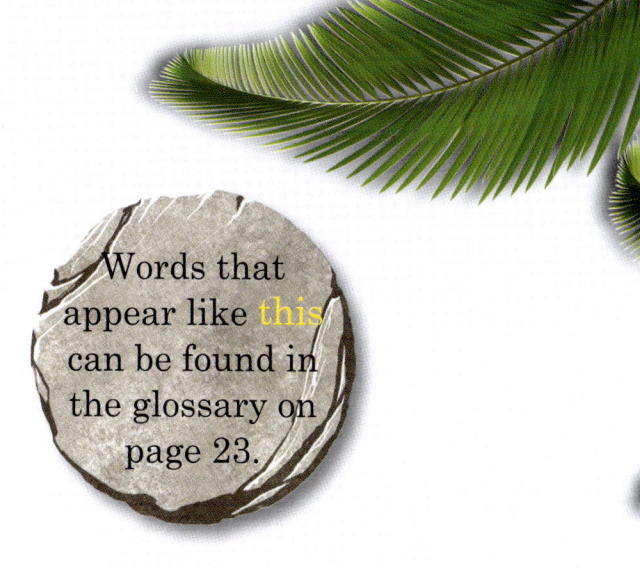

Words that appear like this can be found in the glossary on page 23.

WHAT WERE DINOSAURS?

Dinosaurs were **reptiles** that lived on Earth for over 160 million years before they became **extinct**.

There were many different types of dinosaur. They lived both on land and in water – and some could even fly!

WHEN WERE DINOSAURS ALIVE?

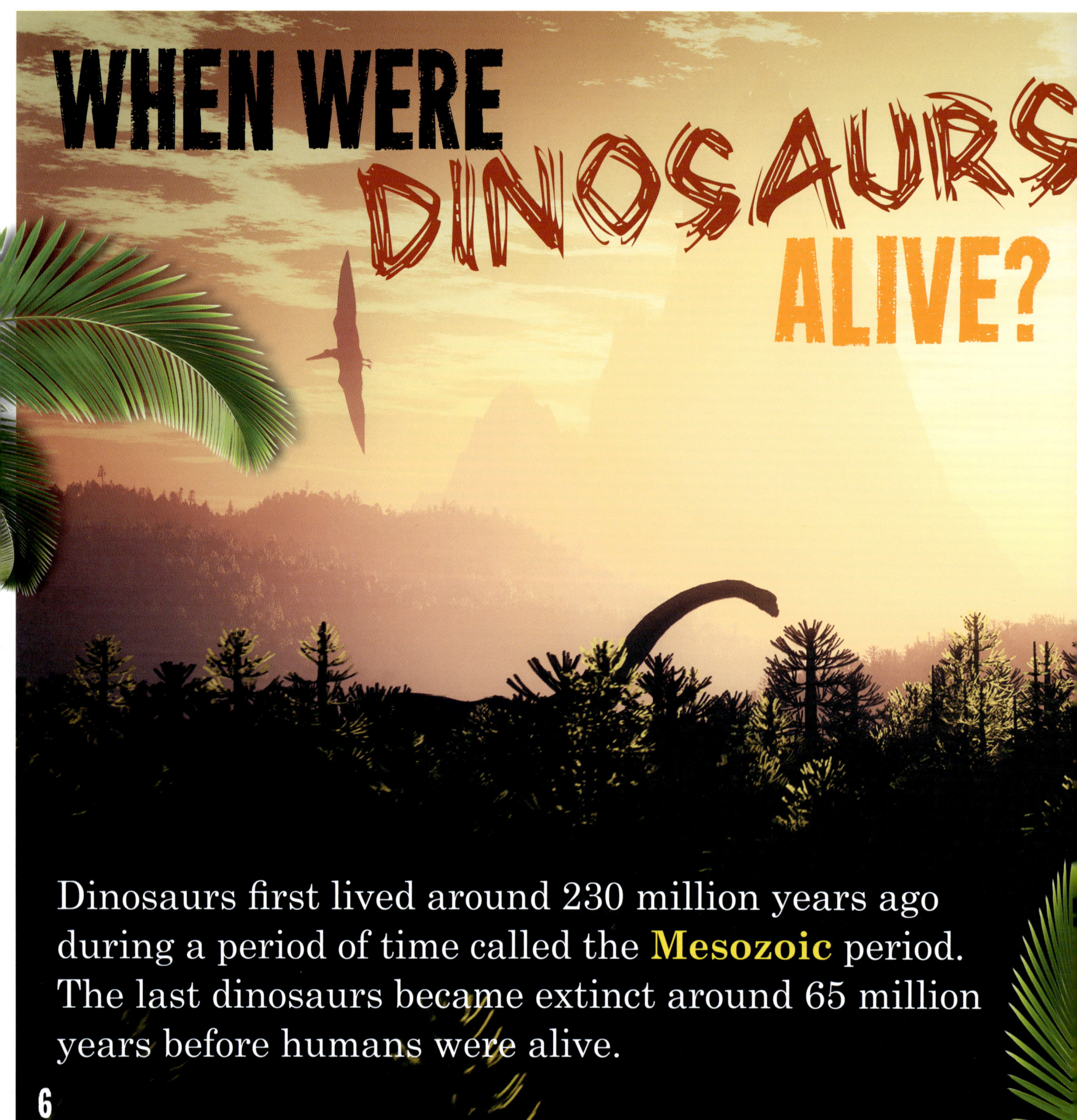

Dinosaurs first lived around 230 million years ago during a period of time called the **Mesozoic** period. The last dinosaurs became extinct around 65 million years before humans were alive.

All land on Earth was together in one piece during the time of the dinosaurs. Over time it has slowly split up into different **continents**.

PANGEA

WHEN ALL THE LAND ON EARTH WAS TOGETHER IN ONE PIECE IT WAS CALLED PANGEA.

TYRANNOSAURUS REX

The Tyrannosaurus rex (ty-ran-o-saw-us rex), also known as the T. rex, was one of the biggest dinosaurs to walk the Earth.

NAME	Tyrannosaurus Rex (ty-ran-o-saw-us rex)
LENGTH	12 metres
WEIGHT	6,000 kilograms
TEETH	60
FOOD	Carnivore
WHEN IT LIVED	65–70 million years ago
HOW IT MOVED	Walked on two legs

The T. rex became extinct around 65 million years ago. There are reptiles today, like the crocodile, that look very similar to the T. rex. However, the T. rex is actually more similar to birds such as chickens and ostriches.

TYRANNOSAURUS MEANS 'TYRANT LIZARD'.

WHAT DID THE TYRANNOSAURUS REX LOOK LIKE?

The T. rex was around 12–15 metres long and 4–6 metres tall. Its head could grow to a massive 1.5 metres long!

We do not know for certain what colour T. rex were, but it is possible that they would have been green to **camouflage** themselves in their **habitat**.

EACH TOOTH WAS UP TO 20CM LONG AND ITS BITE WAS AROUND 3 TIMES MORE POWERFUL THAN THAT OF A LION'S.

WHERE DID THE TYRANNOSAURUS REX LIVE?

The T. rex is thought to have lived in valleys that were covered in trees. The land they lived on is now North America. We know where the T. rex lived because we have found T. rex fossils in these areas.

This means the T. rex could have lived in places other than North America, but their fossils just haven't been found yet.

WHAT DID THE TYRANNOSAURUS REX EAT?

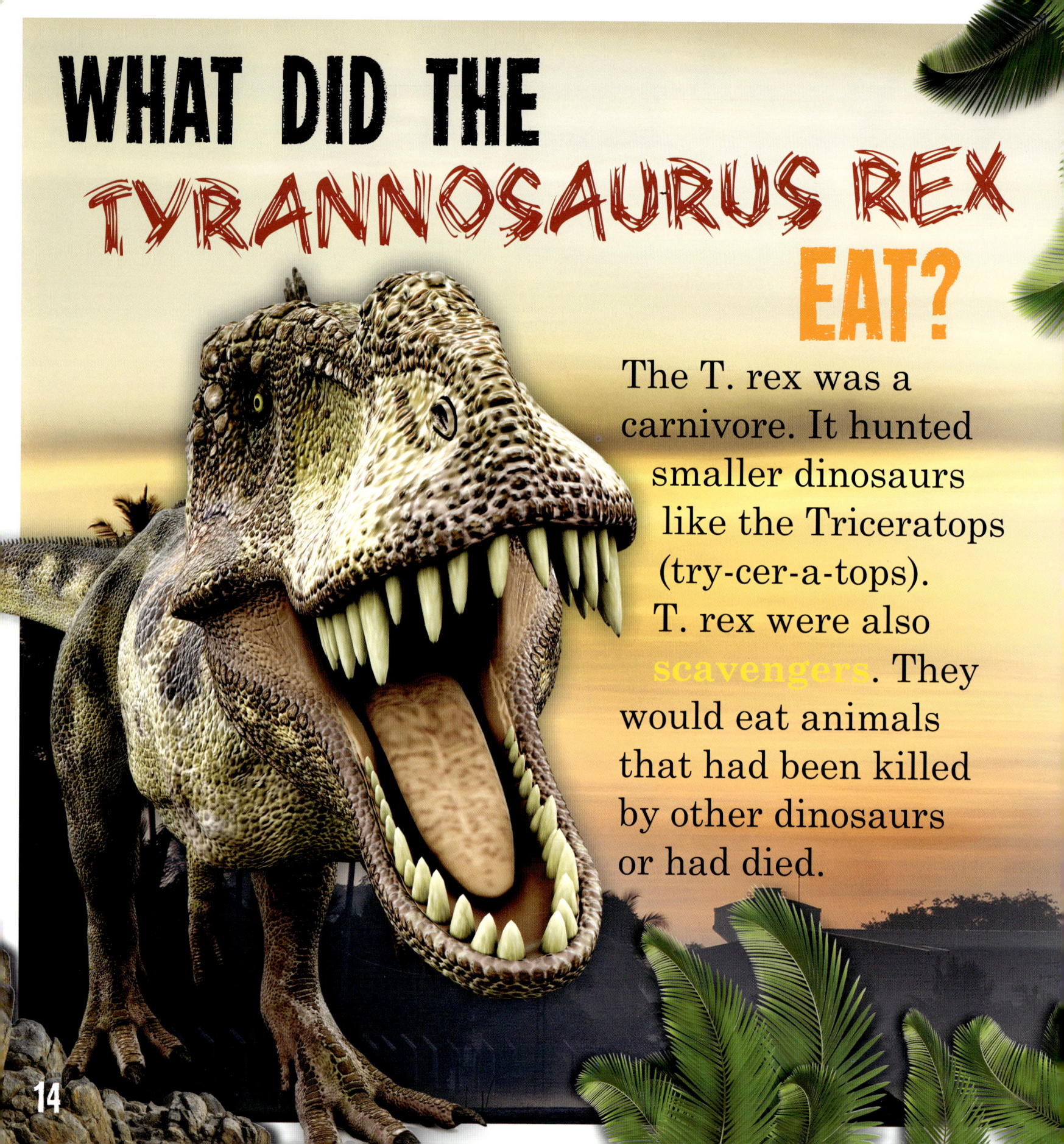

The T. rex was a carnivore. It hunted smaller dinosaurs like the Triceratops (try-cer-a-tops). T. rex were also **scavengers**. They would eat animals that had been killed by other dinosaurs or had died.

Many scientists believe that the T. rex could have eaten up to 230 kilograms of meat in one mouthful. This is about half the weight of an adult horse.

DINOSAURS LIVED ON EARTH FOR 800 TIMES LONGER THAN HUMANS HAVE.

WAS THE TYRANNOSAURUS REX THE BIGGEST DINOSAUR?

The T. rex was one of the biggest predators ever, but it was not the biggest dinosaur that ever lived.

The longest predator was the Spinosaurus (spine-o-saw-us), which could grow up to 18 metres in length. It lived mostly in water, but like a crocodile it could also live on land.

SPINOSAURUS

The tallest dinosaur was the Brachiosaurus (brack-ee-o-saw-us). It could grow to over 15 metres tall.

HOW DO WE KNOW...?

We know so much about dinosaurs thanks to the scientists, called palaeontologists, who study them. They dig up fossils of dinosaurs to find out more about them.

EGG

FOSSIL

Scientists put together the bones they find to try and make the full skeletons of dinosaurs. From these skeletons scientists can often work out the size and weight of a dinosaur. We can also find out information about what it ate from its fossilised food and poo.

↶ SKELETON

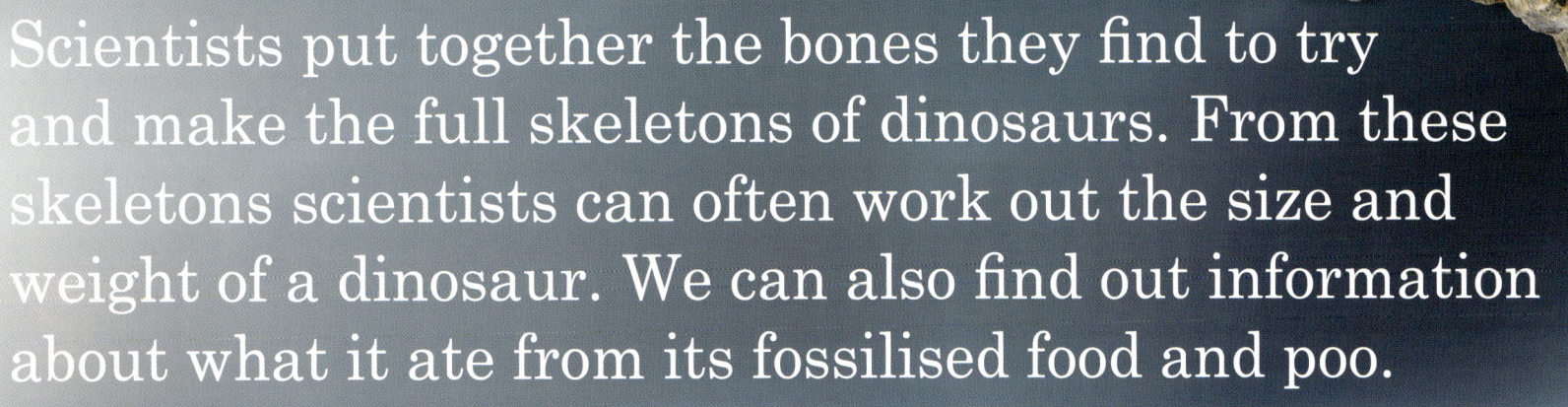

SCIENTISTS EVEN FIND FOSSILISED EGGS AND FOOTPRINTS BELONGING TO DINOSAURS.

FACTS ABOUT THE TYRANNOSAURUS REX

A STRONG AND THICK TAIL THAT WAS USED FOR BALANCE

THEY WEIGHED UP TO 6,000 KILOGRAMS.

POWERFUL BACK LEGS

ITS TEETH GREW BACK AFTER THEY FELL OUT, JUST LIKE SHARKS.

12-15 METRES LONG

1.5 METRE-LONG SKULL

POWERFUL JAWS AND LARGE TEETH

SMALL ARMS

THEY COULD SPRINT AT A SPEED OF NEARLY 20 MILES PER HOUR.

4-6 METRES TALL

THEIR ARMS WERE ONLY AROUND 1 METRE LONG.

DRAW YOUR OWN DINOSAUR

THINK ABOUT THESE QUESTIONS ...
1. How does it move?
2. Does it live on land or in water?
3. What does it eat?
4. What colour is it?
5. How big is it?

GLOSSARY

camouflage — to hide or disguise in a habitat

carnivore — an animal that eats other animals

continents — very large areas of land that are made up of many countries, like Africa and Europe

extinct — an animal that is no longer alive

fossils — the remains of plants and animals that lived a long time ago

habitat — where an animal lives

Mesozoic — a period of time when dinosaurs lived

predators — a type of animal that hunts for food

reptiles — cold-blooded animals with scales

scavengers — animals that feed on other animals that are already dead

INDEX

carnivores 8, 14

crocodiles 9, 16

Earth 4, 7–8, 15

extinct 4, 6, 9

food 8, 14–15, 19

fossils 12–13, 18–19

habitats 11

humans 6, 15

land 5, 7, 12, 16

legs 8, 20

North America 12–13

palaeontologists 18

predators 16

reptiles 4, 9

skeletons 19

teeth 8, 11, 20–21